KU-315-235

THEY THINK
IT'S ALL OVER

EVEN MORE FOOTBALL POEMS

chosen by DAVID ORME

and illustrated by
Marc S. Vyvyan-Jones

MACMILLAN
CHILDREN'S BOOKS

To
Wormbley
Stadium

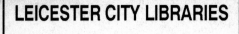

LEICESTER CITY LIBRARIES	
03303533654191	
PETERS	02-Jul-98
J	£2.99

ISBN 0 330 35336 5

This collection copyright © David Orme 1998
Illustrations copyright © Marc S. Vyvyan-Jones 1998

All rights reserved. No part of this publication may be
reproduced, stored in or introduced into a retrieval system, or
transmitted, in any form, or by any means (electronic, mechanical,
photocopying, recording or otherwise) without the prior written
permission of the publisher. Any person who does any unauthorized
act in relation to this publication may be liable to criminal
prosecution and civil claims for damages.

3 5 7 9 8 6 4

A CIP catalogue record for this book is available from the British Library.

Typeset by Macmillan Children's Books
Printed and bound in Great Britain by Mackays of Chatham Plc, Kent

This book is sold subject to the condition that it shall not,
by way of trade or otherwise, be lent, re-sold, hired out,
or otherwise circulated without the publisher's prior consent
in any form of binding or cover other than that in which
it is published and without a similar condition including this
condition being imposed on the subsequent purchaser.

David Orme lives in Winchester and is the author of a wide range of poetry books, textbooks and picture books for children. When he is not writing he visits schools, performing poetry, running workshops and encouraging children and teachers to enjoy poetry.

Marc S. Vyvyan-Jones is better at drawing than playing football, despite hours of coaching from the family dogs, Amy and Kaiya. Marc has illustrated dozens of poetry books and stories, mostly for children, and visits schools to lead workshops which explore the delights of imaginative drawing. He lives and works with his wife Lucy, a writer, in a cottage in Somerset.

0330353365 4 191 62

earwig-o again!

Contents

Kick-off

'Get ready,' says the worm
as the crowd begins to roar.
'Here comes the kick-off
for football book four.

'In between passes
look hard and you'll see
a wriggly little feller –
yup! That's me.'

Tony Mitton

Ten–Nil

The phantom fans are chanting
There's a cheer in my ear as I score:
I've done it again: ten goals to me
And nil to the garage door!

Celia Warren

Dick Tater

I am a little linesman.
I've got a little flag.
Oh, how I love to waggle it.
Wag, wag, wag, wag, wag, wag.

My happiest of memories
(I laughed until I cried!)
Was when that striker
Scored three times,
But I signalled him offside!

(It was curious
To see him so furious.)

John Kitching

Dream Team Song

They're the red vest on the robin
  they're the snowy mountain tops
they're an ocean liner bobbin'
  they're as fast as Keystone Kops
they're the currant in the bun
  and they're hotter
    yes, they're hotter
      yes, they're hotter
        than the sun!

They're the blossom on the cherry
  they're the gifts around the tree
they're the Frenchman's natty beret
  they're the surfer on the sea
they're a fairground filled with fun
  and they're hotter
    yes, they're hotter
      yes, they're hotter
        than the sun!

Wes Magee

Pitch Switch

When you meet me in the street
I'm clumsy on my feet
Is my footwork kinda neat?
No. It's not.

When you haul me back to school
I'm the sort that acts the fool
Thinks he's really cool
But he's not.

When you see me in the town
Pretending I'm a clown
The smartest guy around?
Am I? Not!

But when I'm on the pitch
It's like someone flicks a switch
When I get the ball
I'm all of six foot tall
And when I see the goal
I'm really on a roll
I'm a hero! I'm a giant!
I'm incredible! I'm defiant!
I'm a thousand million billion miles better than the rest!
For all of 90 minutes
I'm the BEST!

Trevor Millum

The World's Most Expensive Footballer

The world's most expensive footballer
has credit cards dripping from his fingertips,
his girlfriend tells of his gold-plated lips,
the studs on his boots have diamond tips.

Pound coins fall from his trouser pocket,
under floodlights he glows like a rocket,
he's electrical with no need of a socket,
he's the world's most expensive footballer.

He throws £50 notes to the crowd like confetti,
his finances tangle like a plate of spaghetti,
he's backed an expedition to seek out the Yeti,
he's the world's most expensive footballer.

He dazzles spectators with his fancy passes,
don't stare at him without wearing sunglasses,
all other players his skill surpasses,
he's the world's most expensive footballer.

Brian Moses

Gran's XI

My grandma's in a football team.
Her age is seventy-eight.
She's no longer like a palm tree
Standing waiting for a date.

The goalie in my grandma's team,
Her age is seventy-four.
Opponents rarely score a goal.
She's built like a grey barn door.

The striker is a real antique,
Captain at eighty-eight.
She's vicious, mean, and fouls a lot;
The kind of striker goalies hate.

Two of Grandma's football team
Are quite acutely deaf.
They shout and wave most rudely
At every weekend ref.

♫ When the red, red robin
Goes 606, bob, bobbing along ♫

Most of Grandma's football team
Have aged, aching bones,
But in the showers, after games,
No single player moans.

ho ho ...

The other week – a rare defeat.
They lost: three goals to five.
But they don't seem to care a lot.
They're just glad to be alive!

John Kitching

Referee, There's a Dog on the Pitch!

'Referee, Referee,
There's a dog on the pitch,'
The player said.

'Referee, Referee,
The dog's dribbling the ball,'
The player cried.

'Referee, Referee,
The dog's won a tackle,'
The player shouted.

'Referee, Referee,
The dog's just been fouled,'
The player yelled.

'Referee, Referee,
The dog's taken a free kick,'
The player screamed.

'Referee, Referee,
The dog's just scored,'
The player growled.

The referee sighed.
He pulled out a red card
And sent the player off.

The team manager substituted another player,
Spot the dog ran onto the pitch
To a tumultuous reception from the crowd
And went on to score the winning goal.

Margaret Blount

The Manager's Lament

'We'll get a result,' the manager said,
'Cos we're comfortable on the ball.
'Pace at the front and sound at the back,
And we make no mistakes at all.'

'We've vision and skill,' the manager said,
'And we play with a flat back four.
Midfield is strong and Jonesy's in form
And our Robbo knows how to score.'

'We'd no luck at all,' the manager said,
When the team had gone down six—two.
'Two goals offside and one was a foul,
And the ref? He hadn't a clue.'

Redvers Brandling

Rainbow Mad

I don't mind
when my ears go red,
when everyone stares
at something I've said.

I don't care
when my fingers turn blue,
when I've missed the bus
and I'm freezing through.

I'm not bothered
when my face looks green,
when I've read horror stories
and think I've seen

vampires and monsters
with slimy purple eyes,
yellow fang-like teeth
five times the normal size.

But I hate it, can't take it,
turn every colour there's ever been,
when I play for our team –
aim at goal . . . and miss.

Joan Poulson

The Start of my Career

I've been picked?
I've really been picked?
You mean I've been picked for the football team?

Pinch me hard.
Wake me up.
Can this be a dream?

No dream!

You've been picked.
You've really been picked.
You have been picked for the football team.

You're the substitute's substitute's substitute
so you'll probably not
get a game.

But we need to know you're ready.
Able. Willing. Keen.
The second eleven might need you.
Come running if we call your name.

Because you've been picked.
You've really been picked.
You have been picked for the football team.

Wow!

Team

James S.
Tinribs
Gopinda
Kaiya
Amy
Olivia
Gaby M.
Thomas
Marianne M.
Anil B.
Andrew
Sub.
Tabitha
Sub. Sub.
Jonesy
Sub. Sub. Sub.
Simon S.

Iron my kit.
Polish my boots.
I'm the substitute's substitute's substitute.

The substitute's substitute's substitute:
I'll probably not
get a game.

The substitute's substitute's substitute:
I'm honoured
all the same.

I'm usually ignored.

But now
    I've been picked

I've sort of
    been picked

I've almost
    been picked

For the Football Team.

(It's a start.)

Bernard Young

Football Strip

They call me Bottomless Barrymore Blue,
I'm famous around the town
for everyone knows, when I kick a ball,
my trousers come tumbling down.

I've tried some old braces knotted with string
but it's the same if ever I score;
I feel a low rumble deep down below
as my trousers slip to the floor.

So I've an idea to help football players
whose trousers don't seem to fit:
just wear a long jumper down to your knees
instead of your old football kit.

Andrew Collett

Exit

50,000

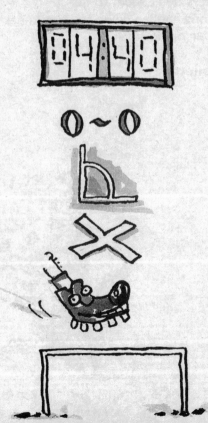

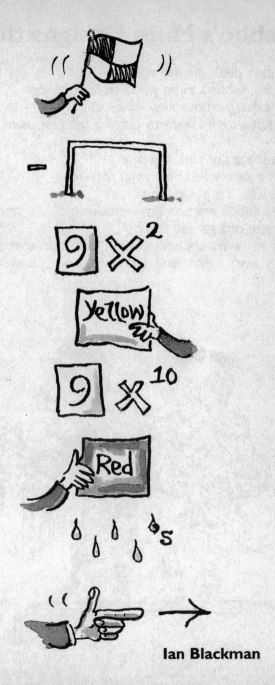

Ian Blackman

Robbo's Mum Designs the Kit

Robbo's dad's the manager
but it's Robbo's mum who's really in charge.
She's designed our new kit . . .
I'm not sure if I want to play for the first team any more.

The shirts are pink and satin
with a yellow and blue petal pattern
There's a frill at the front
and a subtle maroon bow attachment
the size of a garden shrub.
Our numbers are embroidered with luminous sequins
and there's a matching detachable hood just in case it rains.

The shorts are available in a range of corresponding colours:
lemon, lime or raspberry
and the stockings are Lycra
with gold and silver thread
and held up with silk garters that have a rosette motif.

At least there's one thing . . .
we never clash kits with other teams.

Mind you, the platform football boots
were a bit too much.
Even Robbo's dad said we didn't have to wear them
as he adjusted his gold lamé puff-sleeved tracksuit.

Paul Cookson

Desperate for Help

He'd let in 87 goals
With the season still yet young,
And all the fans made fun of him –
His goalie's pride was stung.

So imagine how he must have felt
When a stranger said one day,
'I'll help you, son, I'll soon improve
The standard of your play.'

'Wow,' he said, 'that's great, that's great.
It'll help restore my pride.
Are you a goalkeeper yourself?'
'No – an optician,' he replied . . .

Clive Webster

This Lad's No Fool

He'd applied for a trial with a top football club,
And they'd said, 'Come tomorrow at one.'
He arrived with his kit, all eager and keen,
But alas, the poor lad's brain had gone.

The manager said, 'Can you kick with both feet?'
The lad gave a grin and replied,
'If I kicked with both feet I'd fall flat on my bum,
I'm not stupid.' The manager cried . . .

Clive Webster

My Mum's put me on the Transfer List

On Offer:
one nippy striker, ten years old
has scored seven goals this season
has nifty footwork and a big smile
knows how to dive in the penalty box
can get filthy and muddy within two minutes
guaranteed to wreck his kit each week
this is a FREE TRANSFER
but he comes with running expenses
weeks of washing shirts and shorts
socks and vests, a pair of trainers
needs to scoff huge amounts
of chips and burgers, beans and apples
pop and cola, crisps and oranges
endless packets of chewing gum.
This offer open until the end of the season
I'll have him back then
at least until the cricket starts.
Any takers?

David Harmer

TINRIBS ♥ MILLWALL

Call JONESY for your Building Repairs

Wanted
New MANAGER for England squad. Knowledge of football not essential.

For Sale
Unusual football strip. Stands out well. See Robbo's Dad.

Harry Commentator Says . . .

It's the one we've been waiting for,
It's a game of two halves,
A classic all the way through,
Yet another unique match,
Between two of the best,
With everything to do,
Being put to the test,
At this present moment in time,
With a mountain to climb,
They'll try to close them down in the open,
And open them up at the back,
Keeping it tight in midfield,
And working out some slack,
Looking for a quick goal,
To rock their opponents,
And knock them for six.
At the end of the day,
It's goals that count,
They've got it all to do!
Today,
And every day like it,
And I have to say,
That this unforgettable clash
Between . . . er . . . er . . . er . . . um!

Ian Larmont

New Kit

We were shocked by the colour of our new kit
Which looked like a dog had been sick on it.
It had shirt collars wider
Than the wings of a glider.
The shorts were ankle length – with braces,
The high-heel boots had zips, not laces.

So we made our protest on the football pitch
And played our first game without a stitch.

John Coldwell

Foregone Conclusion

The poor old football manager
Just didn't know what to do –
His team were bottom of the league,
They hadn't got a clue.

He thought, 'Some extra practice
Will do the beggars good.
We'll have a go this Sunday' –
The poor misguided pud.

He got eleven dustbins
And put them all in place,
The normal set-up, 4-4-2,
A smug look on his face.

'Right, lads, all you have to do
Is dribble round each bin,
Push the ball in front of you
And then just shoot it in.'

Alas, the session didn't work,
Despite the extra drill,
The dustbins played his team to death –
And won eleven–nil . . .

Clive Webster

Football Training

Monday
Practised heading the ball:
Missed it – nutted the neighbours' wall!

Tuesday
Perfected my sideline throw:
Fell in the mud – forgot to let go!

Wednesday
Worked on my penalty kick:
A real bruiser – my toe met a brick.

Thursday
Gained stamina – went for jog:
Ran round in circles – lost in the fog!

Friday
Developed my tactical play:
Tackled a goalpost — it got in the way.

Saturday
Exercised — twenty-eight press-ups:
Did pull a muscle — but no major mess-ups.

Sunday
At last — the day of the match,
Came through it all without a scratch.
The ref was amazed how I kept my nerve;
He agreed it's not easy to be the reserve!

Celia Warren

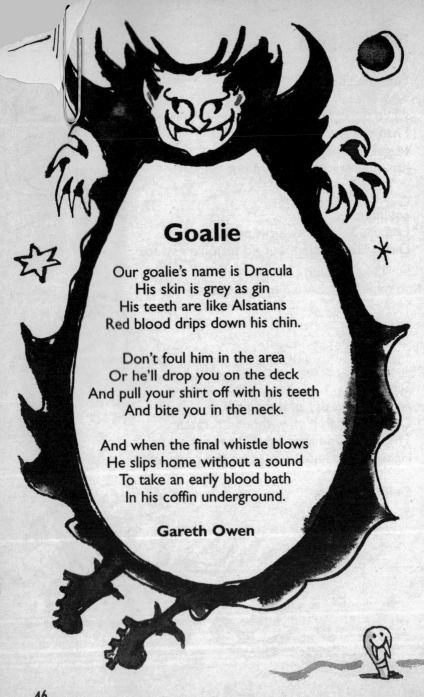

Goalie

Our goalie's name is Dracula
His skin is grey as gin
His teeth are like Alsatians
Red blood drips down his chin.

Don't foul him in the area
Or he'll drop you on the deck
And pull your shirt off with his teeth
And bite you in the neck.

And when the final whistle blows
He slips home without a sound
To take an early blood bath
In his coffin underground.

Gareth Owen

The Stud

I am the stud
who got left in the mud
while the others went home on the boot.
I had the bad luck
to get thoroughly stuck
just as everyone shouted out 'Shoot!'

Our goalscoring ace
fell down flat on his face
as he miskicked the ball and spun round.
He pulled at the sludge
but I just wouldn't budge
so he left me behind in the ground.

So now I'm alone.
Everyone has gone home,
and another stud's taking my place.
I'll stay here stuck fast
dreaming of glories past
till the grass grows and covers my face.

Brian K. Asbury

The Football Family Man

I'm the finest fan
that football's had.
I've a football gran
with a football fad.
I've a football mother
and a football dad.
And my football brother
has football bad.

With my football wife
in our football pad
to our football life
we football add
two football daughters
and a football lad,
all football supporters,
all football mad.

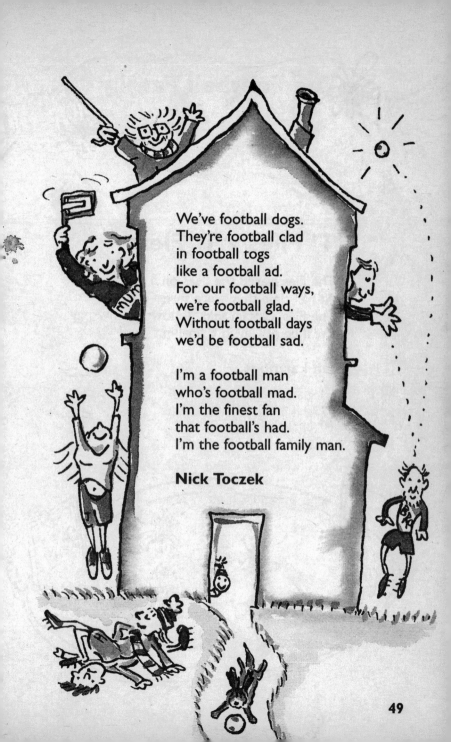

We've football dogs.
They're football clad
in football togs
like a football ad.
For our football ways,
we're football glad.
Without football days
we'd be football sad.

I'm a football man
who's football mad.
I'm the finest fan
that football's had.
I'm the football family man.

Nick Toczek

T' Flies v T' Fleas

The flies played the fleas on a saucer.
At half time they were three—nil up.
The flies' captain said, 'If nowt goes wrong
We'll be playing in t' final in t' cup.'

Ian Larmont

The Grandstand Grans

Eddie's gran and
Sammy's gran,
super-subbing Jammy's gran;

Bazza's gran and
Nicky's gran,
his Auntie Mel with Micky's gran.

They throng along, in hats and scarves,
to watch us every week.
Shouting out
'Away the lads!'
till each can hardly speak.

Robbo's gran and
Rafique's gran
with his cousin Sadiq's gran;

Stewpot's gran and
Andy's gran;
side by side – the Grandstand grans.

Flasks of tea and sandwiches
keep them warm, come rain or shine.
We rarely lose,
now they support –
and the loudest one is mine!

Mike Johnson

Last Word

Said the pitch
to the grandstand,
'I'm old and I'm lined;
Life seems so flat
After all these years.'

Said the grandstand
to the pitch,
'Well, never mind;
I'm so unhappy
My seats are in tiers.'

Trevor Millum

The Night I Won the Cup

Last night I had a wonderful dream,
Dreamed I was the captain of the England football team.
Running on the pitch, feeling ever so proud,
Hearing the roar of the capacity crowd

Shouting, cheering,
Booing, jeering,
Oohing and aahing,
As the game got underway.

It was nearly full-time. There was still no score.
It looked like we'd have to settle for a draw.
From deep in defence we developed an attack.
I jinked and I swerved. I was past their full-back.

And the crowd started shouting:

Whack it! Smack it!
Give it all you've got!
Swerve it! Curve it!
Go on! Take a shot!

The goalie rushed out to do the best he could.
I kept my head down as a striker should.
Into the net, the football soared.
The crowd went mad. Everyone roared.

It's a goal! It's a goal!
He's scored! He's scored!
They were hand-clapping, back-slapping,
Yelling, jumping up.
He's done it! We've done it!
We've won the cup!

I raised my fist to punch the air
And suddenly my dad was standing there
Saying, 'Wake up! Wake up! What's up, our kid?
You sound as if you'd won the cup.'
'Dad,' I said, 'I did!'

John Foster

Final Whistle

The crowd went wild
as the final whistle blew.
But down in his hole
the worm breathed, 'Phew!

'The things they do up there
are quite beyond belief.
Thank goodness it's over.
What a relief!'

Tony Mitton

WE WAS ROBBED
More Football Poems
Chosen by David Orme

Football through the Ages

Football grew from itchy feet
kicking whatever they found in the street;
a pebble; a stick; a rolling stone;
a rusty can or an animal's bone.
The left-over bladder of a butchered pig,
inflated and tied off, was perfect to kick;
if something would roll it would do for the game
that then had not even been given a name
till, on through the ages, the game was to grow,
at long last becoming the football we know.

O, I'm glad of my football, I'm glad of the rules,
I'm glad of the pitches at clubs and at schools,
I'm glad of my kit, but I am even gladder
the days are long gone when they kicked a pig's bladder.

Celia Warren

YOU'LL NEVER WALK ALONE

More football poems
chosen by David Orme

A Perfect Match

We met in Nottingham Forest,
     My sweet Airdrie and I.
She smiled and said, 'Alloa!' to me –
     Oh, never say goodbye!

I asked her, 'Is your Motherwell?'
     And she replied, 'I fear
She's got the Academicals
     From drinking too much beer.'

We sat down on a Meadowbank
     And of my love I spoke.
'Queen of the South,' I said to her,
     'My fires of love you Stoke!'

We went to Sheffield, Wednesday.
     Our Hearts were one. Said she:
'Let's wed in Accrington, Stanley,
     Then we'll United be.'

The ring was Stirling silver,
     Our friends, Forfar and wide,
A motley Crewe, all gathered there
     and fought to kiss the bride.

The best man had an awful lisp.
     'Come Raith your glatheth up,'
He said, and each man raised on high
     His Coca-Cola cup.

The honeymoon was spent abroad:
     We flew out east by Ayr,
And found the far-off Orient
     Partick-ularly fair.

We're home, in our own Villa now,
     (The Walsall painted grey)
And on our Chesterfield we sit
     And watch Match of the Day.

Pam Gidney

Nothing Tastes Quite Like a Gerbil
And other vile verses
chosen by David Orme

Nothing Tastes Quite Like a Gerbil

Nothing tastes quite like a gerbil
They're small and tasty to eat –
Morsels of sweet rodent protein
From whiskers to cute little feet!

You can bake them, roast them or fry them,
They grill nicely and you can have them en croute,
In garlic butter they're simply delicious
You can even serve them with fruit.

So you can keep your beef and your chicken,
Your lamb and your ham on the bone,
I'll have gerbil as my daily diet
And what's more – I can breed them at home!

Tony Langham

A selected list of poetry books available from Macmillan

The prices shown below are correct at the time of going to press. However, Macmillan Publishers reserve the right to show new retail prices on covers which may differ from those previously advertised.

The Secret Lives of Teachers
Revealing rhymes, chosen by Brian Moses

0 330 34265 7
£3.50

'Ere we Go!
Football poems, chosen by David Orme

0 330 32986 3
£2.99

You'll Never Walk Alone
More football poems, chosen by David Orme

0 330 33787 4
£2.99

Nothing Tastes Quite Like a Gerbil
And other vile verses, chosen by David Orme

0 330 34632 6
£2.99

Custard Pie
Poems that are jokes, chosen by Pie Corbett

0 330 33992 3
£2.99

Parent-Free Zone
Poems about parents, chosen by Brian Moses

0 330 34554 0
£2.99

Tongue Twisters and Tonsil Twizzlers
Poems chosen by Paul Cookson

0 330 34941 4
£2.99

All Macmillan titles can be ordered at your local bookshop
or are available by post from:

**Book Service by Post
PO Box 29, Douglas, Isle of Man IM99 1BQ**

Credit cards accepted. For details:
Telephone: 01624 675137
Fax: 01624 670923
E-mail: bookshop@enterprise.net

Free postage and packing in the UK.
Overseas customers: add £1 per book (paperback)
and £3 per book (hardback).